STREET LETHAL

Unarmed Urban Combat

SAMMY FRANCO

PALADIN PRESS
BOULDER, COLORADO

Street Lethal:
Unarmed Urban Combat
by Sammy Franco

Copyright © 1989 by Sammy Franco

ISBN 0-87364-517-0
Printed in the United States of America

Published by Paladin Press, a division of
Paladin Enterprises, Inc., P.O. Box 1307,
Boulder, Colorado 80306, USA.
(303) 443-7250

Direct inquiries and/or orders to the above address.

All rights reserved. Except for use in a review, no
portion of this book may be reproduced in any form
without the express written permission of the publisher.

Neither the author nor the publisher assumes
any responsibility for the use or misuse of
information contained in this book.

Photographs by Levon Andonian and Victor Furnells

Contents

Preface..ix

Introduction 1

Chapter One
    Physical Conditioning 5

Chapter Two
    The Fighting Stance 17

Chapter Three
    The Ranges of Unarmed Combat 27

Chapter Four
    The Offensive Structure 31

Chapter Five
    The Defensive Structure 117

Conclusion 181

To my mother, Barbara Franco, a woman of great courage.

Acknowledgments

I would like to thank the photographers, Levon Andonian and Victor Furnells, for their time and patience in shooting the photos. I would also like to thank Jay Weber, Anthony Fahey, Beverly Franco, and James Phifer, for posing for the photographs.

Thanks to Beverly, Shelli, Audrey, and Dorraine, for their support and encouragement.

Special thanks to Carl Sosebee and Craig Warner for believing in my cause.

About the Author

Sammy Franco has over a decade of experience in the martial arts. He is notably accomplished in theoretical and practical aspects of various eclectic arts, and has received intensive instruction in wing chun gung-fu, bando, kali, and kickboxing.

Through years of study, experimentation, and research, Franco has founded Contemporary Fighting Arts, a modern martial art stressing efficiency and effectiveness. Franco's system is remarkably applicable to the unfortunate violence and danger of modern society.

Sammy Franco has a BA degree in criminal justice from the University of Maryland. His articles on Contemporary Fighting Arts and various self-defense concepts appear in *Inside Karate* and *Inside Kung-Fu* magazines. Franco resides in Silver Spring, Maryland, where he teaches Contemporary Fighting Arts.

Preface

Violent crimes such as homicide, rape, and assault plague our cities and towns. It seems that every time we listen to the news, we hear horror stories. A woman is brutally raped; a man is stabbed to death; a young boy is sexually assaulted. We no longer feel safe in our homes or workplaces; everywhere we turn, there is a threat of violence and danger.

The fear and threat of victimization have caused an evolution of new fighting arts, the "modern martial arts." Such arts were designed to meet the dangers of contemporary society. One of the latest modern martial arts is Contemporary Fighting Arts.

Contemporary Fighting Arts is a highly developed system of self-defense designed to provide effective and efficient skills in unarmed combat. The offensive and defensive techniques of this system have been chosen for their efficiency and destructive potential. Unlike the traditional fighting arts (the ancient martial arts that are still practiced in pure and unaltered form), Contemporary Fighting Arts concentrates on going to the root of a streetfighting situation and quickly settling it. A streetfighting situation is a spontaneous and hostile physical confrontation between two or more individuals where no rules apply. It is a sudden, violent encounter that can occur anywhere, in which anything goes.

This book is merely an introduction to the dynamic essence of Contemporary Fighting Arts; its main purpose is to familiarize the reader with the physical elements of the art (conditioning and the offensive and defensive structures). Unfortunately, it does not cover every aspect of the art. Topics such as strategies, training methods, mental visualization, the psychology of combat, and spirituality cannot be discussed adequately in one book and therefore must be reserved for future volumes.

There is nothing fun or pleasant about streetfighting. It is dangerous, unpredictable, and usually unfair. But most importantly, it is a reality that all of us must come to grips with. I hope that you will never have to fight for your life. But if you do, you will stand an excellent chance of survival if you have trained diligently and absorbed the material in this book.

Introduction

Having studied the fighting arts for well over a decade, I have noticed a slow, yet progressive, change in the martial arts world. It seems that the martial arts community has divided into two opposing schools of thought. The first school of thought is that of the "traditional" martial artists; the second is that of the more eclectic "modern" martial artists.

The first group consists of orthodox martial artists who train and fight using systems and techniques that were developed in sixteenth-century China and other ancient, Eastern settings. To this day, these martial artists practice their fighting art in its pure and unaltered form. They believe there is no need to change or modify their style of combat, for what worked in the past will work in the present. If one is to preserve and maintain the authenticity of a martial art, then the style must not be changed in any way, shape, or form. According to the traditionalists, modification of a system is heresy.

Traditional martial artists are well known for their showmanship. They often can be seen at tournaments performing powerful breaking techniques, flawless kata, and complex weapon drills. These demonstrations are impressive and easily attract the attention of spectators. After all, such feats require tremendous skill and years of dedicated training.

Yet these ornamental shows do not display the actual *fighting* proficiency of an effective martial artist. It is an unfortunate fact that most traditional techniques are too complex and impractical for encounters on our modern city streets. Much of what is appropriate for exhibitions and tournaments simply is not practical or applicable on the urban battlefield.

The traditional martial arts do have their place for people whose interests lie in the cultural, spiritual, and theatrical aspects of the fighting arts. Nonetheless, a clear distinction between reality and fantasy must be made when it comes to unarmed combat.

On the other side of the spectrum are the modernists. They are unorthodox in their approach to the fighting arts in that they believe in conformity for the sake of progression. In other words, they believe that if a martial artist is to remain functional and survive, he must change and adapt to the demands of the present environment.

Unlike traditionalists, modern martial artists are not great showmen. Their techniques and maneuvers are not overly complex or fancy. They stress efficiency and effectiveness in terms of destructive potential. These eclectic, modern fighters are concerned only with the functional concepts of the combat arts, and their training is geared primarily for the streets.

To gain proficiency in modernistic styles and skills, the martial artist must study and train in a modern school that teaches a modern system. One such system is Contemporary Fighting Arts.

Contemporary Fighting Arts is a progressive martial art

Introduction

designed for the individual who desires a more effective style of combat. It is a system that is geared for dangerous city streets or any place where "gentlemanly" rules of fighting do not exist. The system focuses on effective and efficient tools of destruction.

There are three vital elements to Contemporary Fighting Arts: mental, physical, and spiritual.

The Mental Element

This is the cognitive element of Contemporary Fighting Arts; how to approach unarmed combat in a logical and strategic manner. Combat strategies include: fighting different somatotypes, multiple opponents, environmental strategies, and assessing the opponent's strengths, weaknesses, style, and conditioning. Techniques of mental visualization play a major role in developing the practitioner's mind. Other styles and systems are researched and analyzed for strengths and weaknesses, and the martial artist is urged to develop a hunger for knowledge of the fighting arts.

The Physical Element

This is the most demanding aspect of Contemporary Fighting Arts and requires *total* commitment from the practitioner. He must fully condition his body by developing his cardiovascular endurance, muscular strength, and flexibility, and by maintaining a proper diet and nutritional habits. A well-seasoned fighter is in excellent physical shape; it is that plain and simple.

Through diligent training in the offensive and defensive structures of Contemporary Fighting Arts, the martial artist will develop and sharpen his combat skills until maximum speed, power, and accuracy are achieved. He will also possess the ability to fight any opponent at any range, something that few traditional schools teach.

The Spiritual Element

Through the spiritual element of Contemporary Fighting Arts, the martial artist's combative spirit is recognized and then cultivated. He learns to identify and accept the way of the warrior.

Meditative practices also play a big role in the development of the warrior's spirit. Meditation calms the soul, creates inner peace, reduces stress, and promotes patience. All of these qualities are essential to the serious martial artist.

* * * * * * *

Together, these three elements constitute the nucleus of Contemporary Fighting Arts. Each element is equally important, for one cannot function without the other. The mental, physical, and spiritual elements are developed to promote change and adaptation to new circumstances and situations.

By developing and teaching Contemporary Fighting Arts, I may be accused of heresy by many traditional martial artists. Yet I stand prepared to be judged by only modern martial artists.

Chapter One

Physical Conditioning

Physical conditioning is one of the most neglected aspects of a martial artist's training regimen. Conditioning can make all the difference between winning and losing a streetfight. Physical conditioning encompasses the maintenance of cardiovascular strength, muscular strength, general flexibility, and a low level of body fat. All of these qualities are essential for a well-prepared martial artist.

Cardiovascular Strength

Your body's cardiovascular system is comprised of your heart, lungs, and circulatory system. When in a fight, your cardiovascular system comes under a tremendous amount of stress. Therefore, like any muscle, your heart and lungs must be strengthened to be able to respond well in a violent situation. This requires aerobic exercises.

Aerobic comes from the Greek term meaning "with air." For any exercise to be considered aerobic, it must be performed uninterrupted so the heart rate remains elevated for thirty to forty minutes. This should be done at least four times per week. Aerobic exercises include running, rope

Physical Conditioning

skipping, cycling, swimming, and rowing. These activities will help the fighter improve his wind capacity, endurance, stamina, circulation, and muscle tone.

Muscular Strength

The next important element of physical conditioning is the development of muscular strength. Muscular strength is the maximum amount of force a muscle can exert in a single effort. Muscular strength is critical to the martial artist because it promotes power and speed. If you want to develop strength, you must progressively overload and stress your muscles.

Free weights seem to be the most popular form of strength training today. They are available in most gyms or can be purchased at a sporting goods store for home use. Be sure to execute all free-weight exercises in a slow and controlled manner—hoisting and jerking the weights only leads to injury. If you are not familiar with the various exercises, ask a competent instructor for assistance. Most commercial weight sets for home use include instruction manuals and exercise tips.

Nautilus machines arrived in the early 1970s. The machines were designed to isolate and strengthen specific muscle groups. Many martial artists prefer training on Nautilus equipment because it does not give them that bulky appearance that often results from free-weight training. The biggest drawback to Nautilus is the expense—you would most likely have to join a gym or spa to gain access to the machines.

Calisthenics

As an alternative to working out with free weights or

Physical Conditioning

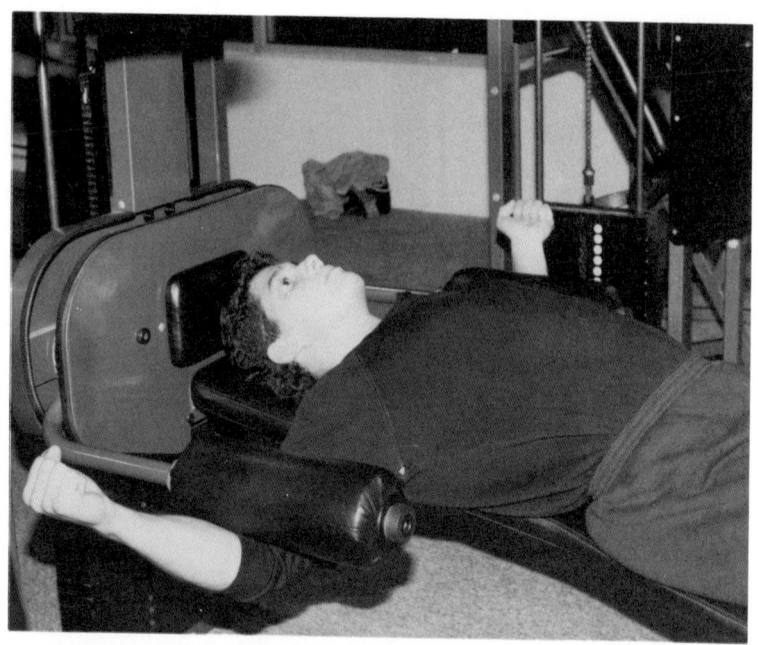

Physical Conditioning

Nautilus, try calisthenics. Calisthenics are simple yet effective exercises performed without special equipment. The fighter uses his own body weight as resistance while doing the exercises. These exercises include sit-ups, push-ups, squat thrusts, chin-ups, and pull-ups.

Flexibility

It is imperative that a well-rounded fighter be flexible as well as strong. *Flexibility* is a muscle's ability to move through its entire natural range of motion. To develop and increase flexibility, the martial artist should perform various stretching exercises.

There are numerous reasons why the martial artist should stretch his muscles. First, stretching before your workouts will greatly reduce the chance of pulling or

Physical Conditioning

straining your muscles. Second, stretching helps relax tense muscles, which in turn improves the speed of your techniques. Finally, stretching promotes better body awareness and increases the muscle's range of motion.

Stretching exercises are very easy to learn and can be performed at home. Be sure to hold each stretch for a minimum of thirty seconds. You may experience mild discomfort, but under no circumstances should you feel pain. Avoid bouncing movements when stretching, as this can cause muscle strains and tears.

Low Level of Body Fat

Being overweight can greatly inhibit the performance of a martial artist. If you are overweight, your combat techniques will usually lack speed and explosiveness, your

Physical Conditioning

mobility will be limited, and you will often prematurely run out of breath in a combat situation. Therefore, a low level of body fat is essential if you are to become a fast and fearsome fighter. To achieve this, you must perform your aerobic exercises in conjunction with a nutritionally balanced diet. When I speak of diet, I am referring to a *lifestyle* of eating right, not a specific weight-loss scheme.

To begin, we must no longer think of our bodies as flesh and bone but rather as a machines of combat, or war machines if you will. To properly fuel these machines, one must consume the proper foods. Therefore, the pugilist must be very conscientious of *what* and *how much* he eats.

Seventy percent of the fighter's daily caloric intake should come from complex carbohydrates, which are the body's primary source of energy. They can be found in vegetables, fruits, potatoes, pastas, and various grain products.

The next 20 percent of his daily calories should come from proteins. Proteins are responsible for the growth and maintenance of muscle and cell tissue. Poultry, fish, legumes, and various milk products are all good sources of protein.

The final 10 percent of the warrior's daily intake should come from unsaturated fats. Fats are an excellent source of energy and are vital for proper body functioning. Unsaturated fats can be found in nuts, seeds, and grain products.

Nutritional supplements should also be taken to ensure that the pugilist is receiving all of the necessary vitamins and minerals in his diet.

By following these guidelines, and with a bit of discipline, the martial artist can easily and safely create a body that is worthy of unarmed combat.

Chapter Two

The Fighting Stance

A proper fighting stance is essential for effective self-defense because it is the foundation from which the fighter executes his offensive and defensive techniques. The key to the fighting stance is the centerline.

The centerline is an invisible, vertical line that divides your body in half. It begins at the top of the head, runs down the center of the torso, and ends at the groin. It is significant because your most vital targets are located along this imaginary line—the eyes, nose, throat, sternum, solar plexus, and testicles.

If you become involved in a fight, you must make a conscious effort not to directly expose your centerline to your opponent. This is accomplished by learning a proper fighting stance. I have found this particular stance to be excellent for unarmed combat because it offers sufficient protection to your centerline, yet it does not restrict your ability to attack an assailant.

Unlike the traditional boxer's stance, the martial artist places his strongest and most coordinated side forward. Thus, a right-handed fighter stands with his right hand and right foot forward. If you feel that your left side is your

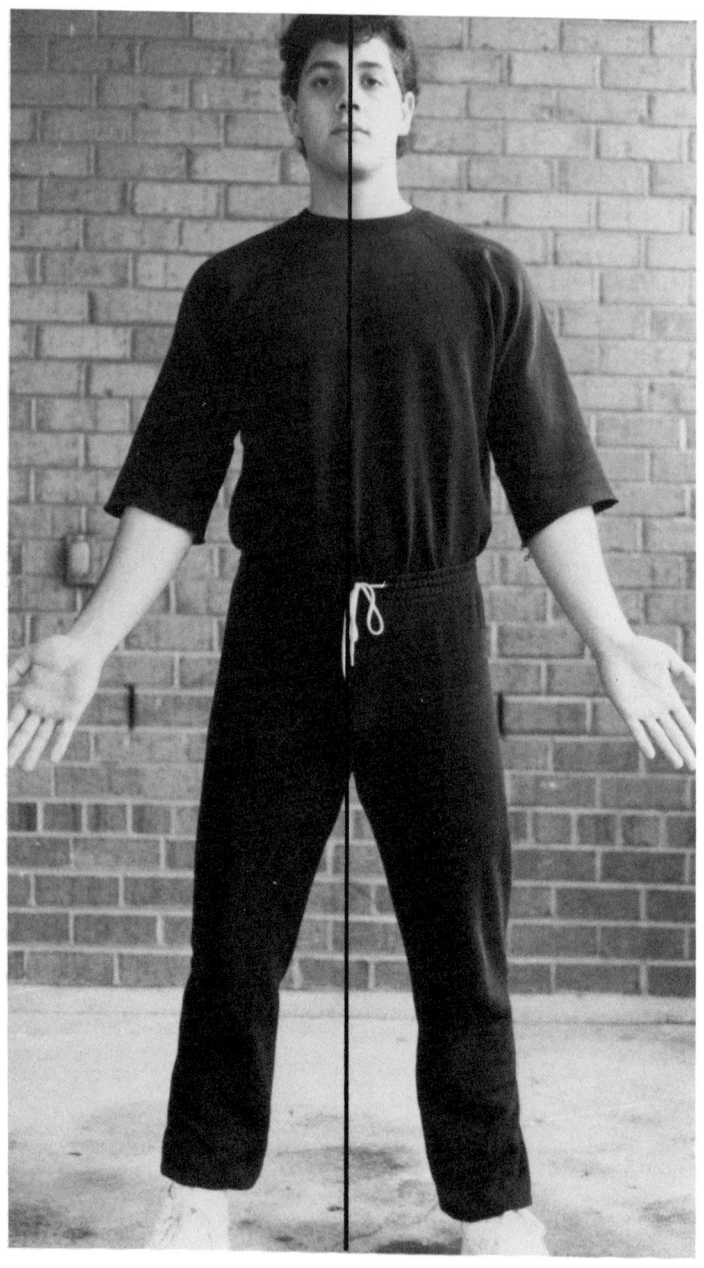

A proper fighting stance.

strongest side, however, then by all means you should lead with it.

When assuming this fighting stance, always have both knees slightly bent in a semi-relaxed position. Your feet should be placed at a 45-degree angle from the opponent. This situates your centerline at a protective angle from the assailant. It is especially important that your lead foot is turned slightly inward to protect your groin region. Your rear heel can be raised or flat, whichever you prefer. It is a good idea to have it raised slightly, however, to facilitate a springlike explosion toward your assailant.

During actual combat, your weight distribution is going to change constantly; but when starting out in the fighting stance, have 50 percent of your weight on each leg. Be balanced and relaxed—*but be ready!*

Your hand positioning is another important part of your stance. Your lead arm should be held up high and bent between 90 and 120 degrees, while your rear arm is kept back in front of your chin for defensive purposes. The lead arm is used primarily for attacking, though the rear arm can also be used to attack an opponent. Your arms should be held in a relaxed position, yet prepared to instantly attack the adversary. This relaxation will increase the speed of your offensive techniques.

The boxer's and wrestler's stances shown in the photographs are frequently used during unarmed combat, but they are poor choices for streetfighting. Notice the direct foot positioning, which directly exposes the centerline. Primary targets are open for an attack.

The cat and horse stances are popular among many karate and kung-fu stylists, but they, too, are poor choices for unarmed combat. The cat stance is a poor choice due to its narrow foot positioning. Mobility is hindered because there is too much weight placed on the rear leg. Conse-

The Fighting Stance

These photographs demonstrate the proper way to position your hands. Notice how the martial artist's hands are relaxed but ready. His hands are also a good distance apart. The lead arm is extended while the rear hand is kept close to his chin.

This photograph displays the incorrect way to position your hands. The fighter's hands are too tense and rigid, which will only retard the speed of his punching tools. His hands are also too close together—the lead arm needs to be further extended while his rear hand should be held higher.

The Fighting Stance

The wrestler's stance.

The boxer's stance.

The horse stance.

The cat stance.

quently, a punch thrown from this stance will have little power because of the lack of weight on the front leg. The hand positioning is too low, leaving the martial artist's head vulnerable to an attack.

The horse stance is a poor fighting stance because of its *wide* foot positioning, which directly exposes the martial artist's centerline and hinders his mobility. It is also virtually impossible to defend against an attack with one hand extended and the other placed on the hip.

Chapter Three

The Ranges of Unarmed Combat

Before we discuss the offensive tools for unarmed combat, the reader must first be aware of the three ranges of unarmed combat. These are the three separate distances from which you can engage an opponent. These distances are known as kicking range, punching range, and grappling range. It is essential that the practitioner become proficient in all three ranges.

Kicking Range

The furthest distance of unarmed combat is known as *kicking range*. At this distance, the martial artist is too far from his opponent to apply hand techniques, so he would use his legs to strike.

Punching Range

The mid-range distance of unarmed combat is termed *punching range*, where the martial artist would use his hands to attack an opponent.

Grappling Range

The final and closest distance of unarmed combat is *grappling range*. At this range, the martial artist is too close to his opponent to strike him with his hands, so he would use tools like elbows, knees, gouges, and other close-quarter techniques.

Kicking range.

The Ranges of Unarmed Combat

Punching range.

Grappling range.

Footwork

Mobility is one of the most important aspects of fighting. When attacking, it enables you to move through the ranges of unarmed combat and overwhelm the opponent with a flurry of blows. When combined with your defensive tools (blocks, parries, and slipping maneuvers), mobility allows you to safely avoid the assailant's attack.

Moving quickly and efficiently can be achieved through proper basic footwork. This does not mean dancing around like a professional boxer. Such fancy movements will only waste precious energy and leave you vulnerable to an attack. Footwork means quick, economical steps that are performed on the balls of your feet, while you remain relaxed and balanced.

Basic footwork is structured around four different movements:

Moving forward—From a fighting stance, move your lead leg forward (about 12 inches) and let your rear leg follow an equal distance. To advance more quickly, you can push off your rear foot.

Moving backward—From a fighting stance, step back with your rear leg (about 12 inches) and let your lead leg follow an equal distance.

Sidestepping right—From a fighting stance, quickly move your right (lead) leg to the right (8 to 12 inches) and let your left (rear) leg follow an equal distance.

Sidestepping left—From a fighting stance, quickly move your left (rear) leg to the left (8 to 12 inches) and let your right (lead) leg follow an equal distance.

Chapter Four

The Offensive Structure

The objective of the offensive structure is to quickly incapacitate the opponent through the application of offensive techniques. These techniques have been chosen for their efficiency and destructive potential. For reasons of simplicity and organization, I have categorized each offensive tool into one of the three possible ranges of combat.

It is important to mention that a martial artist should never use fancy or complex techniques when he is involved in a streetfight. Such ornamental techniques are just too risky and inefficient for the practitioner. What may have worked for Bruce Lee in the movies might not work for you in the streets. A distinction between fantasy and reality must be made.

One important, but often overlooked, aspect of unarmed combat is the fighter's state of mind. Physical ability is not the only element of combat; the mind and body must learn to harmonize with each other to complete the desired task. When the martial artist decides to execute his attack, he must do so with *total* commitment—anything less can lead to disaster. He must not become preoccupied with silly notions of winning or losing. His mind must be calm and clear so his offensive attack will be effective.

The martial artist must also learn to become more aggressive and ruthless than his assailant. When the fighting begins, you must transform into a savage beast who will rip his prey apart without the slightest feelings of remorse. It is this frame of mind that will lead to your survival in a streetfight.

Kicking Range Tools

Kicking techniques separate a martial artist from any common boxer, wrestler, or brawler. They give the martial artist a strong advantage over his assailant. Kicks will:

- Allow you to strike your opponent from a safe distance.
- Cause your opponent to drop his hand guard, thus allowing you to strike his facial targets (i.e., eyes, nose, temple, throat, and chin).
- Permit you to hit your assailant's targets with great speed and surprise.
- Allow you to safely close the distance gap between you and the opponent.
- Keep multiple attackers at bay.

It is no wonder that so many pugilists choose to apply kicks in a streetfight.

All kicks, regardless of their style or origin, can be divided into two categories. The first group is known as *high-line* kicks while the second is identified as *low-line* kicks.

High-line kicks are kicking techniques that are directed to targets above the opponent's waist level, such as the head, chest, ribs, and kidneys. Low-line kicks are kicking tools that are designated for targets below the opponent's waistline, like the hip, groin, thigh, kneecap, and shin.

High-line kicks are very impressive and can really please a crowd of spectators, but their functional application in a streetfight is dubious. They are just too risky and inefficient for the streets.

Anytime you throw a high-line kick in a fight, you drastically increase your chances of falling off balance. This is especially true if you are standing on a slippery surface, such as wet pavement, ice, mud, or sand (keep in mind that the martial artist must use combat techniques that can be applied on any type of surface under any environmental conditions).

Being able to execute a high-line kick is also dependent on the type of clothing you are wearing at the time of a fight. Would you be able to kick an opponent in the head if

In this photo, Franco demonstrates a typical high-line kick. These types of kicks are too risky to be used in a streetfight.

you were wearing tight jeans, a full length coat, or a tailor-made suit? Finally, high-line kicks require much more energy to execute compared to low-line kicks, and conserving one's energy is vital in a streetfight.

The martial artist must therefore resort to using low-line kicks. When performed properly, they can be very damaging. I can verify, from my own personal experience, that one accurately placed kick to the opponent's knee can quickly end a fight. Low-line kicks are excellent for streetfights because they are quick, deceptive, and very efficient.

Vertical Kick

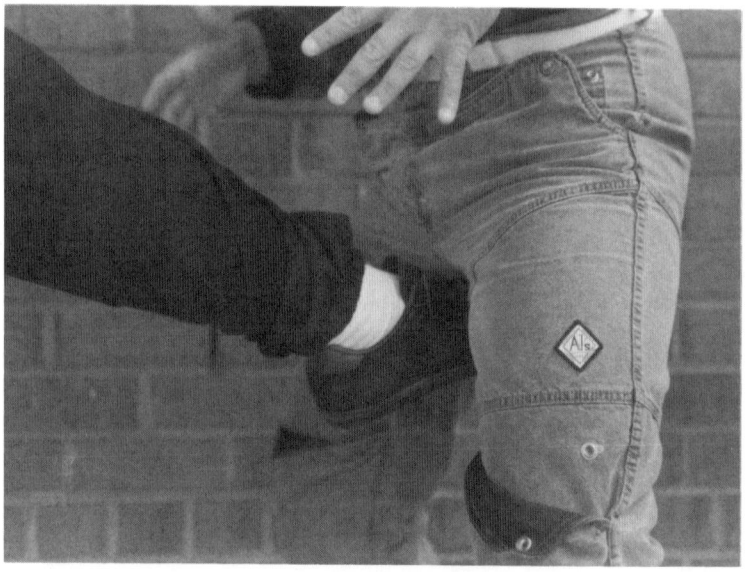

The vertical kick is one of the quickest kicks in your arsenal. This kick can be delivered from many angles. Your target is the opponent's groin, specifically his testicles. Contact should be made with the instep of your lead foot. A strong kick to a man's groin can cause shock, vomiting, and even unconsciousness.

The Offensive Structure

Franco (right) squares off with his opponent.

Without any telegraphic movement, he snaps his lead leg into his opponent's groin region.

Now that the assailant is distracted, the pugilist can finish him off.

Knee/Shin Kick

This is a devastating kick aimed at your assailant's knee or shin. Contact is made with the heel of your foot. This kick is also excellent for closing the gap between you and your opponent.

The Offensive Structure

Franco squares off with his opponent.

With a quick shuffle, the shin kick is delivered. Notice how the pugilist leans away from his opponent when the kick is performed.

Push Kick

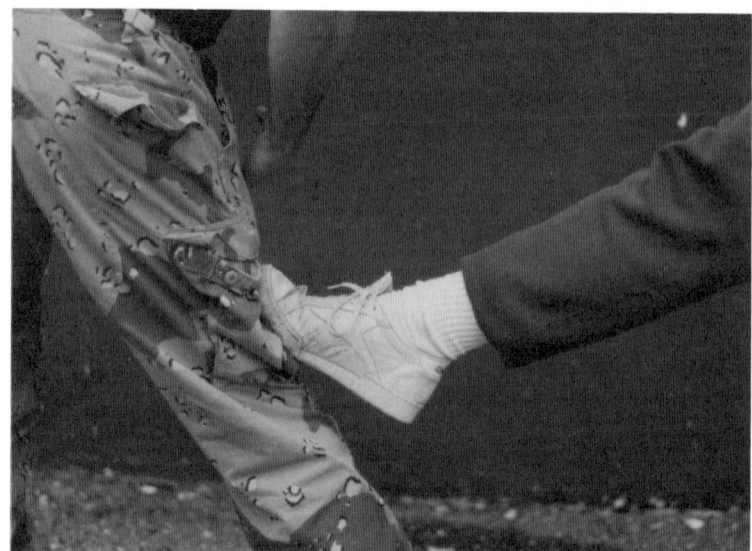

This is a very powerful kick that is thrust into the opponent. The kick is executed with your lead leg, and contact is made with the ball of your foot. Your target is the assailant's hip, thigh, knee, or shin.

To execute a push kick, Franco quickly thrusts his lead foot into his opponent's thigh.

Hook Kick

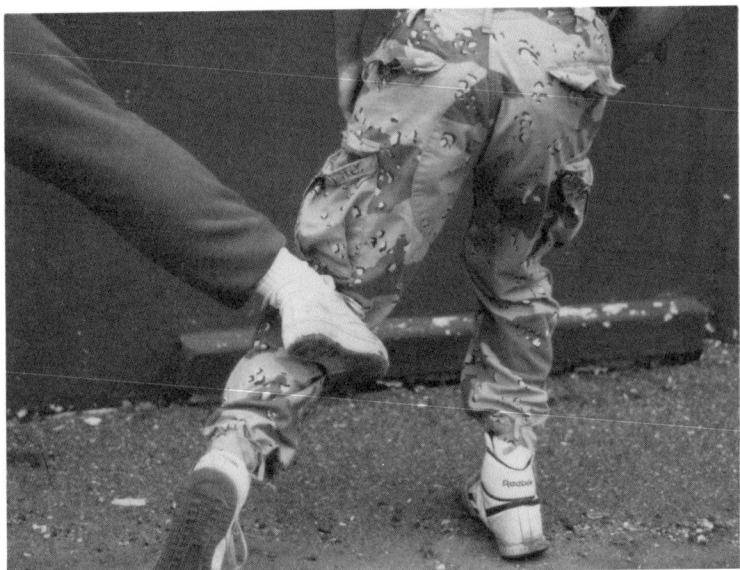

This is a powerful kick that is thrown with your rear leg. By torquing your hip, you can generate a tremendous amount of force. Your target is the back or side of the opponent's knee or thigh.

With a quick torque of the hip, Franco executes a hook kick.

The opponent is easily knocked off balance.

He topples to the ground, where Franco can finish him off.

Side Kick

The mechanics for the side kick are similar to that of the knee/shin kick. This kick is extremely powerful and is almost always guaranteed to knock your opponent on his tail. The side kick is targeted for the opponent's hip, waist, or thigh. Contact is made with the heel of your foot.

As the assailant rushes in, Franco launches a side kick to his hip.

Punching Range Tools

Of the three ranges of unarmed combat, punching range is the most efficient for the martial artist. This is because the offensive tools used in this range (e.g., finger jabs, rear crosses, and hooks) do not require a lot of energy to execute, yet they can inflict a tremendous amount of damage on the opponent.

It is essential that the martial artist strike the assailant with as much power as possible. To put sufficient power behind your punches, you must learn to throw your body weight into every blow and remember to aim your strike *through* the opponent. Contact should be made with the center knuckle of your fists. Proper breathing is also very important. Never hold your breath; rather, learn to exhale when you deliver your blows.

Whenever executing a punch, you must always remember to keep your wrist straight. Imagine your fist and forearm as a solid pipe that cannot bend in any direction. Only your elbow should bend when you throw punches.

If all of these guidelines are kept in mind and your blow is delivered with sufficient speed, you will be able to knock an opponent out rather easily.

Finger Jab

This is by far the most effective punching-range tool that you can use in a fight. The objective of the finger jab is to impair the opponent's vision by striking his eyes with your fingertips. The finger jab's most amazing quality is that it requires only a small amount of energy to execute, but produces a tremendous amount of damage to the opponent.

Franco is faced with an opponent.

By quickly extending his lead arm, the finger jab reaches its destination.

The Offensive Structure 45

The opponent's vision is now impaired.

The finger jab is an offensive tool that can be used by anyone of any size. It is especially helpful to people who are not strong enough to deliver a bone-crushing blow.

A young woman sits in the park awaiting the arrival of her friend.

The man sitting next to her decides to show his true intention.

Having no other choice, the girl quickly executes a finger jab into her attacker's eyes.

The attacker is quickly incapacitated, allowing the woman to escape safely.

Lead Straight

The lead straight is a punch that is thrown with your lead arm. It is a quick punch because it travels in a linear direction toward the opponent. Remember, the shortest distance between two points is a straight line. Initial contact should be made with your middle knuckle. Your principal target is the opponent's head.

Franco squares off with his opponent.

Without a second's hesitation, the lead straight is whipped out.

Rear Cross

The rear cross is the heavy artillery used in punching range. Like the lead straight, the rear cross travels in a straight line toward the opponent. Power is generated by quickly pivoting your rear foot and hip. The rear side of your body functions much like the hinge of a swinging door. Your target is the opponent's head.

Franco starts out in a fighting stance.

The martial artist drives a rear cross into his opponent's face.

Lead Hook

The lead hook can be a devastating blow if it is performed properly. The punch is thrown with your lead arm and travels in a circular direction toward the opponent's head or body.

To execute the lead hook, you must pivot your lead hip and foot into the blow while simultaneously whipping your arm in the direction of the assailant. A common mistake is to "wind up" or chamber your hook before you throw it. Such actions will only telegraph your intentions to the opponent. When throwing a lead hook, remember to keep your rear hand up in case your attacker decides to counter your blow.

With a quick pivot of his lead hip, Franco executes a lead hook from a fighting stance. Note that Franco does not wind up before throwing the punch.

The Offensive Structure

Rear Hook

The rear hook is much like the lead hook, but it is delivered with your rear arm. When throwing a rear hook, remember to pivot your rear foot and hip into the blow while simultaneously whipping out your bent arm. When performing hooking techniques, it is important to keep your wrists straight to avoid injury.

The two opponents square off.

With a quick twist of the hip, the rear hook is thrown.

Lead Uppercut

The lead uppercut is another punishing blow that is thrown with your lead arm. To properly deliver the uppercut, you must shift your weight to the front of your body while lifting your lead heel from the floor. Your lead arm should travel in a vertical direction to the opponent's chin or body.

In one fluid motion, Franco drives a lead uppercut into his opponent's ribs.

The wind is knocked out of the assailant.

Rear Uppercut

The rear uppercut is executed with your rear arm and can be performed by shifting your body weight to the lead side while raising your rear heel off the ground. Once again, your rear arm travels in a vertical direction.

The two fighters square off.

Franco launches a rear uppercut into the opponent's solar plexus.

Lead Shovel Hook

The body mechanics for this technique are identical to that of the lead uppercut except that your lead arm travels at an angle to the opponent's ribs rather than in a straight vertical direction.

Franco squares off with the opponent.

He suddenly drives a lead shovel hook into the opponent's ribs.

Rear Shovel Hook

The body mechanics of this technique are identical to that of the rear uppercut except that your rear arm travels at an angle to the opponent's ribs.

Franco squares off with the opponent.

He then drives a rear shovel hook into the opponent's ribs.

Grappling Range Tools

Grappling range is often thought of as being the distance at which only wrestling techniques can be applied. To the contrary, there are numerous striking tools that are at the pugilist's disposal, many of which are more damaging than any wrestling lock or hold. Tools such as elbow strikes, knee strikes, and gouges are direct, efficient, and can easily be employed against any opponent of any size.

Due to the close proximity of the opponent, grappling range is considered to be the most dangerous distance of unarmed combat and should be approached with caution.

Elbow Strike

The elbow strike is considered to be the most devastating offensive technique in the streetfighter's arsenal. This strike is so quick and powerful it is almost impossible to stop. Elbow strikes are also great tools for getting out of locks and chokes. Targets are the head, throat, solar plexus, ribs, and kidneys. There are three different types of elbow strikes: vertical, horizontal, and reverse.

Vertical Elbow Strike

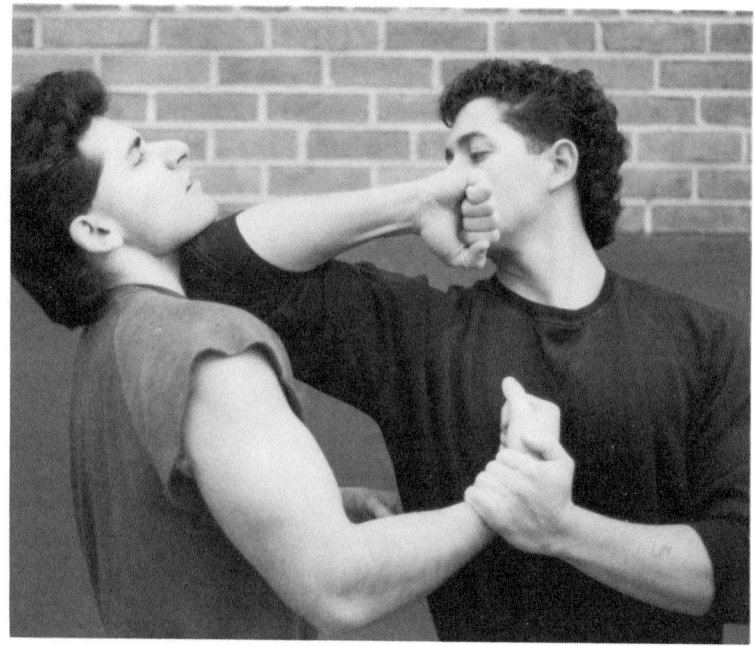

The vertical elbow travels vertically to the opponent's chin, throat, or body. It can be performed off either the left or right side of the body. The power for this strike is acquired through the quick extension of the legs at the moment of impact.

The Offensive Structure

Franco is grabbed by his opponent and is forced to fight at grappling range.

He quickly counters with a vertical elbow to the chin.

The results are obvious.

Horizontal Elbow Strike

This strike travels horizontally toward the assailant's head or torso. To generate power for this strike, you must forcefully pivot your hips and shoulders in the direction of the opponent.

Franco is grabbed by the opponent.

With a quick pivot of his hips, the martial artist cracks his attacker in the jaw.

Reverse Elbow Strike

This strike is used when one is placed in a choke or hold from behind. The reverse elbow strike travels in the reverse direction of the horizontal elbow.

The opponent sneaks up on Franco and puts him in a hold. Franco acquires his balance and prepares to deliver his counter.

With a quick twist of his hip, Franco drives his elbow into his opponent's jaw.

The Offensive Structure

He moves in to finish the fight.

Knee Strike

The knee strike is another powerful grappling-range tool. Its targets are the groin, solar plexus, and head. When using a knee strike, make contact with your kneecap and avoid making contact with your quadriceps.

Vertical Knee

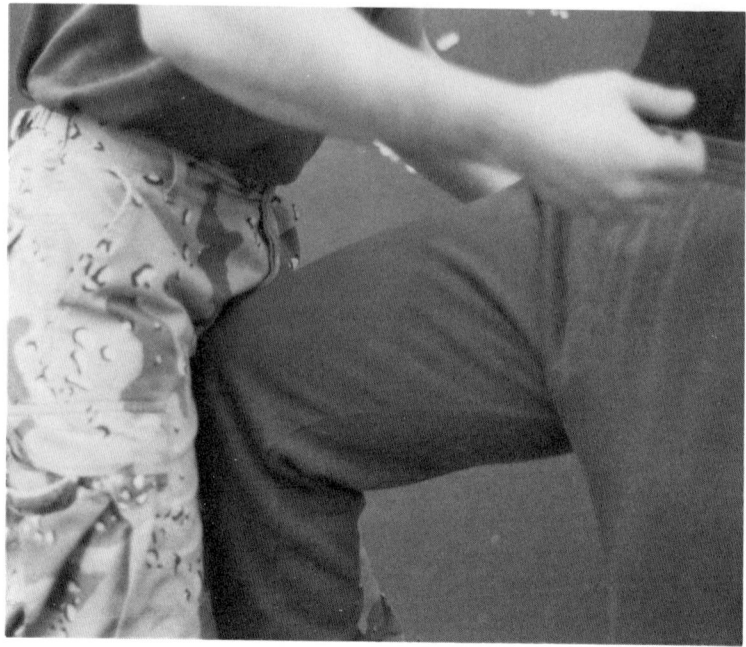

The vertical knee travels in a vertical direction toward the opponent's vital targets. The blow can be initiated off either leg.

The Offensive Structure

Franco is grabbed by the opponent.

He grabs his opponent's arms so that he can balance himself and simultaneously initiates a vertical knee to the groin.

Horizontal Knee

This knee strike travels on a horizontal plane toward the opponent, much like a hook kick. Your targets are the head, ribs, and hips. Remember to make contact with your kneecap. This strike can also be thrown off either leg.

The Offensive Structure

Franco is placed in a throat choke.

Without a moment's hesitation, he pulls his opponent off balance and drives a horizontal knee into the ribs.

Double Thumb Gouge

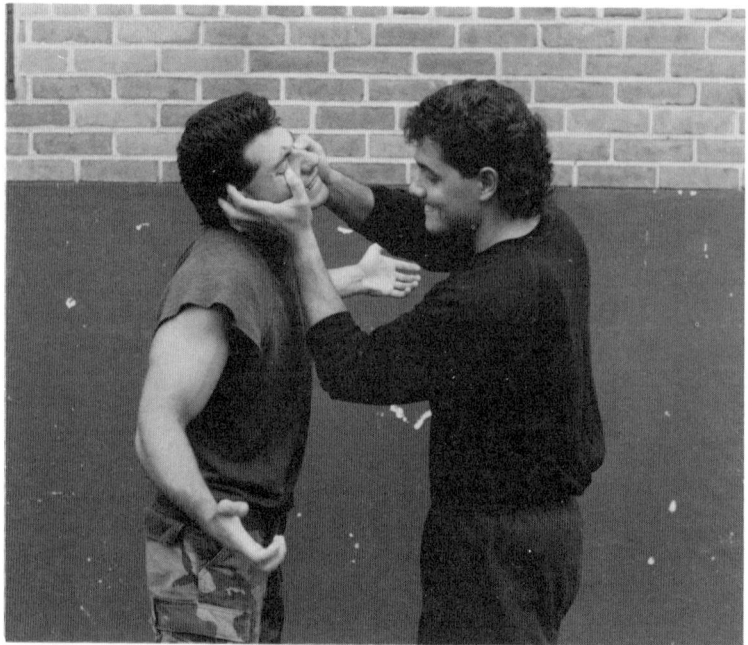

The double thumb gouge is another close-quarter tool that is well known for its effectiveness. To perform the gouge, the martial artist places both hands on either side of the opponent's face and instantly drives his right and left thumbs into his eyes. Temporary blindness, shock, unconsciousness, and even permanent blindness may result. This technique has proven to be fatal. It therefore should be used only in life-or-death situations.

The Offensive Structure

Franco is confronted by an opponent at grappling range.

Without telegraphing his intentions, he moves in with a double thumb gouge.

The opponent falls to the ground in a state of shock.

The Offensive Structure

Biting Tactics

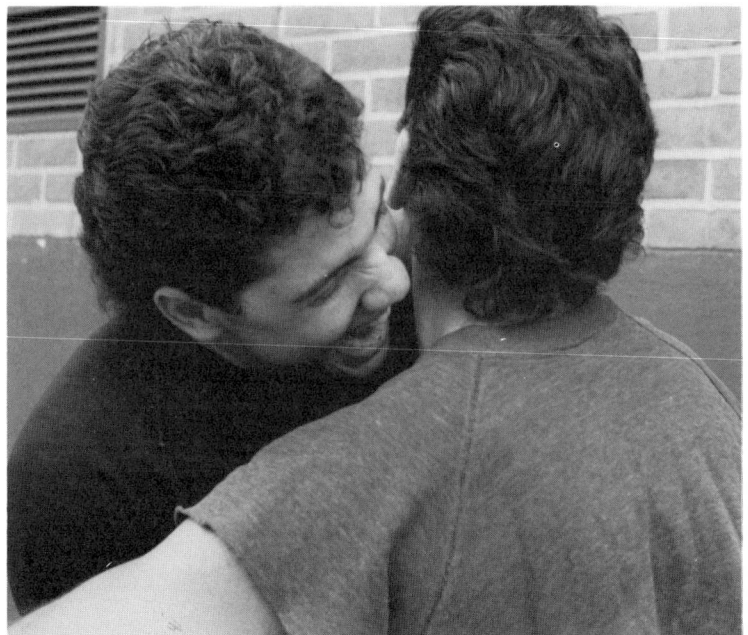

Biting is an excellent deterrent to an opponent who attempts to wrestle with you. Biting is extremely painful and almost guaranteed to make him release his choke, lock, or hold. Some key targets are the nose, ears, throat, fingers, arms, and legs. Biting tactics require extreme ruthlessness. Be warned, however; you run the risk of contracting AIDS if your opponent is infected with the disease and you draw blood while biting him.

Franco is placed in a bear hug.

Immediately, he bites into the assailant's neck.

The Offensive Structure

The opponent releases his hold. Franco is now ready to attack.

Head Butt

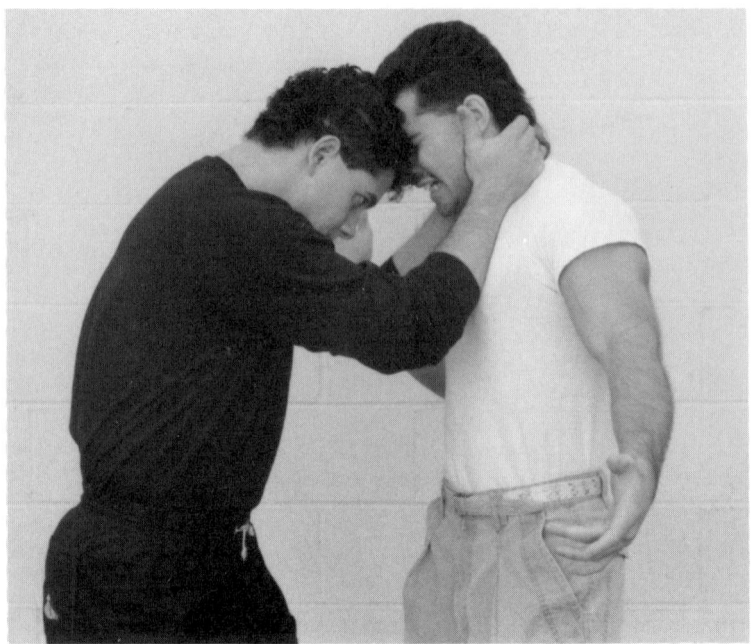

Another close-quarter tool that has the capability of knocking out almost any attacker is the head butt. Like biting, the head butt can be applied when your arms are pinned or trapped by the assailant.

To deliver the blow properly, cock your head back and quickly snap it forward to the bridge of the opponent's nose. Contact should be made with your forehead.

The Offensive Structure

Franco is faced with an opponent at grappling range.

He grabs the opponent's head and pulls him into a head butt.

Foot Stomp

The foot stomp is a great distraction tool. This grappling-range tactic is known for breaking toes as well as causing excruciating pain for the recipient. This technique is performed by forcefully stomping on the opponent's toes with the heel of your shoe.

The Offensive Structure

Franco is faced with an opponent at grappling range.

He forcefully stomps on the assailant's toes.

The opponent drops his hands. Franco can now move in with a strike.

Compound Attacks

Whenever two or more techniques are thrown in succession it is known as a compound attack. A good example of this would be a compound side kick/finger jab/left hook/right uppercut.

It is interesting to know that compound attacks cause more knockouts than any single technique. A compound attack is much more difficult to defend against because it overwhelms the opponent with a flurry of blows.

The most important aspect of the compound attack is your initiating technique. It functions as a distracting device that drops the opponent's guard and throws him off balance. Once the opponent drops his guard, you should be able to effectively land the rest of your blows.

The following sequences of techniques demonstrate some strategic compound attacks.

The Offensive Structure

Shin Kick/Finger Jab/Rear Hook

Franco starts off in a fighting stance.

With a quick shuffle, he delivers a shin kick to the opponent's left leg.

After the adversary drops his guard, Franco delivers a finger jab strike.

He then finishes the fight with a rear hook to the head.

The Offensive Structure

Push Kick/Rear Cross/Lead Uppercut

Franco's attack begins with a powerful push kick to the opponent's lead thigh.

Once the opponent drops his guard, Franco throws a rear cross.

He follows with a lead uppercut to the chin.

The Offensive Structure

Hook Kick/Rear Cross/Foot Stomp

Franco starts off in a fighting stance.

He quickly executes a hook kick to the assailant's thigh.

Once the opponent drops his hands, Franco drives a rear cross to the chin.

He ends the fight with a foot stomp to the ribs.

The Offensive Structure

Vertical Kick/Rear Cross/Lead Straight/Rear Uppercut

With a quick snap of his lead leg, Franco executes a vertical kick to the opponent's groin.

He then follows through with a rear cross to the face . . .

. . . followed by a lead straight.

The opponent is finished off with a rear uppercut to the chin.

The Offensive Structure

Knee Kick/Horizontal Knee/Horizontal Elbow

Franco starts off in a fighting stance.

His attack begins with a knee kick to the opponent's lead leg.

He then moves into grappling range with a horizontal knee to the ribs.

The opponent is finished off with a horizontal elbow to the jaw.

Once the opponent is distracted, Franco moves in with a vertical knee to the face.

The opponent falls to the ground and can be finished off with a foot stomp to the ribs.

The Offensive Structure

Finger Jab/Vertical Knee/Foot Stomp

Franco starts off in a fighting stance.

Without any telegraphic movement, he delivers a finger jab strike to the opponent's eyes.

Lead Straight/Rear Cross/Lead Hook/Rear Hook

Franco steps in with a lead straight to the opponent's face . . .

. . . followed by a rear cross.

He then delivers a lead hook . . .

. . . and finishes the opponent off with a rear hook to the temple.

The Offensive Structure

Lead Straight/Rear Shovel Hook/Lead Hook

Franco starts off in a fighting stance.

He snaps a lead straight to the opponent's face.

He then delivers a rear shovel hook to the body.

The opponent is finished off with a lead hook to the head.

Finger Jab/Rear Cross/Lead Straight/Rear Uppercut

Franco's compound attack begins with a finger jab to the eyes.

Once the opponent's vision is impaired, he delivers a rear cross.

He then follows with a lead straight.

The opponent is finished off with a rear uppercut.

The Offensive Structure

Finger Jab/Rear Hook/Lead Hook/ Rear Uppercut/Lead Uppercut

Franco starts off in a fighting stance.

His attack begins with a finger jab to the eyes.

Once the opponent is distracted, Franco delivers a rear hook to the jaw.

He then delivers a powerful lead hook . . .

The Offensive Structure

... followed by a rear uppercut to the chin.

The opponent is finished off with a lead uppercut.

Low Feint/Finger Jab/Rear Cross/Horizontal Knee

To draw the opponent's attention away, Franco feints low.

He then quickly throws a finger-jab strike . . .

The Offensive Structure

... followed by a rear cross.

Franco then grabs the opponent's hair and pulls him into a horizontal knee strike.

Foot Stomp/Head Butt/Vertical Knee

Franco is faced with an opponent at grappling range.

To distract the opponent, he delivers a stomp to the foot.

The Offensive Structure

Now that the opponent's attention is taken, Franco grabs his head and pulls him into a head butt.

The adversary is finished off with a vertical knee to the face.

Horizontal Elbow/Vertical Elbow/Vertical Knee

Franco is confronted by an opponent at grappling range.

He immediately attacks the assailant with a horizontal elbow to the temple.

The Offensive Structure

Once the adversary is dazed, Franco delivers a vertical elbow to the chin.

The opponent is finished off with a vertical knee.

Double Thumb Gouge/Vertical Knee/Head Butt

Franco starts off in a fighting stance.

Once the opponent gets close enough, Franco attacks him with a double thumb gouge.

The Offensive Structure 115

He delivers a vertical knee to the groin.

The opponent is then pulled into a head butt.

Chapter Five

The Defensive Structure

The ability to defend against an opponent's attack is of the utmost importance. It is defense that offers protection for the martial artist. Unarmed combat is not always going to be an offensive encounter; defensive skills are vitally important and frequently utilized. Remember, you cannot deploy your forces if the castle is under siege.

The defensive tools that will be discussed in this chapter are blocks, parries, and slipping maneuvers.

Blocks

The most fundamental defensive tools are blocks. The block functions as a barrier to stop an opponent's circular attack (e.g., hook, uppercut, roundhouse kick, or crescent kick). I can assure you that good blocks are very reliable and are capable of withstanding the most powerful of strikes.

There are four different types of blocks that are used in unarmed combat—high blocks, medium blocks, low blocks, and the leg block.

High Blocks

High blocks are applied whenever the assailant attempts to deliver blows to your head. The block is performed by raising either one of your arms over your head to meet the force of the opponent's strike. Contact should be made with the meat of your forearm.

The Defensive Structure

Medium Blocks

Medium blocks are designed to stop punches and kicks that are targeted for the lower portion of your head as well as the upper portion of your torso. The block can be performed by simply raising either one of your arms at a 90-degree angle to catch the impact of the attacker's strike.

Low Blocks

Low blocks are employed when the opponent attacks the lower portion of your torso. A low block is performed by dropping either forearm down to stop the opponent's low strike (e.g., uppercut or shovel hook).

The Defensive Structure

The Leg Block

The leg block is a defensive tactic that is employed whenever an opponent attacks with a low-line kick. It works well against foot sweeps, hook kicks, vertical kicks, shin kicks, and the like. The block is performed by raising your lead knee to meet the assailant's oncoming kick. Contact should be made with your shin or instep.

Parries

Parries are slightly different than blocks. They are used to *redirect* an assailant's linear blow (e.g., jab, cross, or sidekick). A parry is like a quick, forceful slap. An effective parry will almost always throw the opponent off balance, which will permit you to easily counter his attack. There are three main types of parries: inward, outward, and downward.

Inward Parry

The inward parry is performed by simply moving either hand horizontally across your body to deflect the opponent's linear blow. Contact should be made with the palm of your hand. The technique is called an inward parry because your hand travels from the outside in.

The Defensive Structure
Outward Parry

The outward parry is similar to the inward parry except that your hand travels from the inside out. Contact is made with the back of your hand.

Downward Parry

The downward parry is performed by moving either hand in a vertical direction to deflect the opponent's linear low blow. Once again, contact should be made with the palm of your hand.

Slipping

Slipping is the most efficient defensive maneuver. Slipping means avoiding the opponent's punch or kick without moving out of range. The maneuver is utilized against linear blows.

Slipping can be accomplished by leaning backward, sideways, or downward to avoid a blow. Slipping is sometimes preferable over blocking because it throws the opponent off balance and leaves both your hands free to counter. After successfully slipping an opponent's technique, you should immediately attack any exposed target.

The Defensive Structure

Slipping Backward

Start off in a fighting stance. The instant the opponent throws his technique, lean your head back far enough for the opponent to miss.

Slipping Sideways (to the right)

Start off in a fighting stance. Quickly sway your head and upper torso to the right to avoid the opponent's blow.

Slipping Sideways (to the left)

Start off in a fighting stance. Quickly sway your head and torso to the left to avoid the opponent's punch.

Slipping Downward

Start off in a fighting stance. When the opponent throws his punch, bend at the knees and lower your target under the opponent's blow.

Defending Against Punches and Kicks

This section will show the reader how to apply his defensive tools against an opponent's attack. Along with showing the proper defensive technique, it will also demonstrate the most effective counterstrike. These counterstrikes are *not* the only ones possible; there are many variations, and it is up to the pugilist to decide on the best one for the moment. The following sequences are only examples of the many options open to you.

The Defensive Structure

Defense Against a Lead Straight

When the opponent throws his punch, Franco slips to the left.

He counters with a lead straight to the face . . .

. . . followed by a rear shovel hook to the opponent's ribs.

Defense Against a Rear Cross

The assailant throws a rear cross. Franco parries it with his right hand (inward parry) . . .

. . . and counters with a rear cross.

He then pulls the opponent into a horizontal knee.

The Defensive Structure

Defense Against a Right Hook

The opponent throws a right hook. Franco intercepts it with his left arm (medium block)...

...and counters with a finger jab to the opponent's eyes...

. . . followed by a rear cross.

The Defensive Structure

Defense Against a Left Hook

The opponent throws a left hook. Franco blocks it with his right arm (medium block)...

...and counters with a rear cross...

. . . followed by a lead shovel hook to the ribs.

The Defensive Structure

Defense Against a Left Overhead Punch

The assailant throws a left overhead punch. Franco blocks it with his right arm (high block) . . .

. . . and counters with a rear cross to the face.

Defense Against a Right Low Punch

The opponent throws a low punch. Franco parries it and simultaneously counters with a lead straight...

...followed by a rear hook to the assailant's head.

The Defensive Structure

Defense Against a Shin Kick

The opponent attacks with a shin kick. Franco uses a leg block to deflect the kick . . .

. . . and counters with a rear cross.

Defense Against a Vertical Kick

When the opponent throws his kick to the groin, Franco blocks it with a leg block.

He counters with a finger jab . . .

The Defensive Structure

. . . followed by a rear cross.

Defense Against a Front Thrust Kick

When the opponent executes a front thrust kick, Franco parries it with his right hand (downward parry).

Once the opponent's leg touches the ground, Franco counters with a kick to the knee.

The Defensive Structure 143

The opponent is finished off with a rear cross to the head.

Defense Against a Foot Sweep

The opponent tries to sweep Franco's feet from under him. Franco raises his lead knee.

He then counters with a rear cross to the assailant's face.

The Defensive Structure

Defense Against a Right Roundhouse Kick

The adversary throws a right roundhouse kick to Franco's head. He blocks it with his left arm (medium block)...

...and counters with a hook kick to the base leg.

The opponent topples to the pavement.

The Defensive Structure

Defense Against a Left Roundhouse Kick

The attacker throws a left roundhouse kick to the head. Franco blocks it with his right arm (medium block).

He counters with a knee kick to the base leg.

The opponent falls to the ground in pain.

The Defensive Structure

Defense Against a Side Kick

The opponent attacks with a side kick. Franco parries it with his right hand (downward parry)...

...and counters with a hook kick to the opponent's lead leg.

Franco then finishes him off with a rear hook to the head.

The Defensive Structure

Defense Against a Right Crescent Kick

The opponent attacks with a right crescent kick to the head. Franco blocks it with his left arm (medium block) . . .

. . . and counters with a lead straight to the chin.

Defense Against a Left Crescent Kick

This time the opponent attacks with a left crescent kick. Franco blocks it with his right arm (medium block) . . .

. . . and counters with a vertical kick to the groin.

The Defensive Structure

The opponent doubles over, and Franco finishes him off with a rear uppercut to the chin.

Defense Against a Spinning Backfist

The opponent begins to execute a spinning backfist.

Franco blocks the attack and simultaneously counters with a lead straight to the jaw . . .

The Defensive Structure 155

. . . followed by a leg sweep.

Defense Against a Spinning Side Kick

The opponent throws a spinning side kick to the head. Franco quickly slips to the right...

...and counters with a rear horizontal elbow to the opponent's throat...

... followed by a lead horizontal elbow.

Defending Against Locks, Chokes, and Holds

Being placed in a throat choke, or any restraint technique for that matter, can be a startling experience for the fighter. In most situations, it is not the choke, lock, or hold that defeats the pugilist; it is the panic. For this reason, a martial artist should always remain relaxed so he can quickly assess the situation and respond accordingly.

Once placed in a choke or hold, the practitioner must react *immediately*, before his attacker can apply any significant amount of pressure. One rule of thumb is to never match muscle against muscle by forcefully wrestling your way out of the restraint. This will only waste your time and energy and may even enhance the effect of the opponent's technique. All you need to escape are a few powerful strikes to one of the opponent's exposed targets. If he has you in a hold or choke, then his hands will most likely be occupied—he will therefore be unable to defend against your counterattack. Execute your counterattacks as efficiently as possible, and remember: conservation of energy is vital when streetfighting.

Defending Against a Wrist Grab

Franco is confronted by a hostile man.

The Defensive Structure

The opponent grabs his wrist and prepares to initiate a strike.

Franco quickly counters with a rear cross to the opponent's face.

Defending Against a Front Hug (arms free)

Franco is grabbed from the front with his arms remaining free.

He instantly counters with a brutal double thumb gouge to the assailant's eyes.

The Defensive Structure

He then follows with a vertical kick to the groin.

Defending Against a Front Hug (arms pinned)

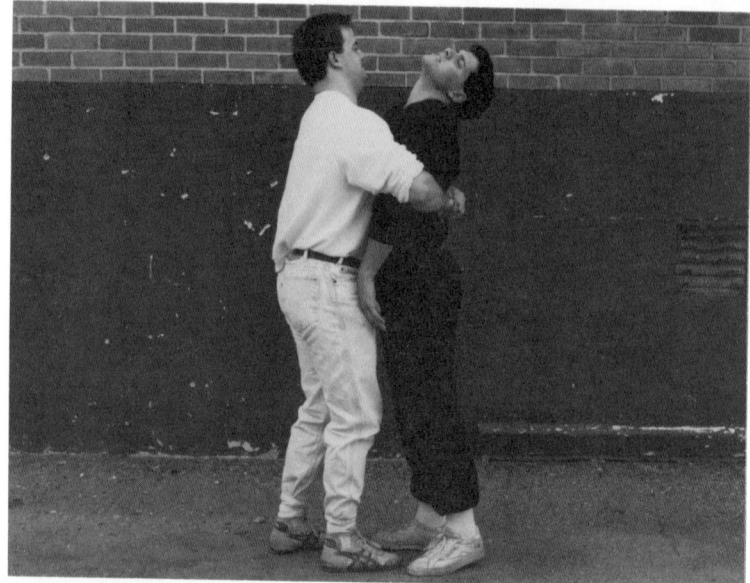

Franco is grabbed from the front with his arms pinned at his sides.

He quickly counters with a head butt to the opponent's nose . . .

The Defensive Structure

. . . followed by a rear hook to the temple.

Defending Against a Rear Hug (arms free)

Franco is placed in a rear hug with his arms remaining free.

He delivers a reverse elbow strike to the attacker's head.

The Defensive Structure

165

The opponent falls to the ground in pain. Franco can now finish him off.

Defending Against a Rear Hug (arms pinned)

Franco is placed in a rear hug with his arms pinned at his sides. Before the opponent can apply maximum pressure, the martial artist reaches back and strikes the assailant's groin.

The opponent has no other choice but to release his hold (above). Franco then launches a finishing blow to the head with a vertical knee (below).

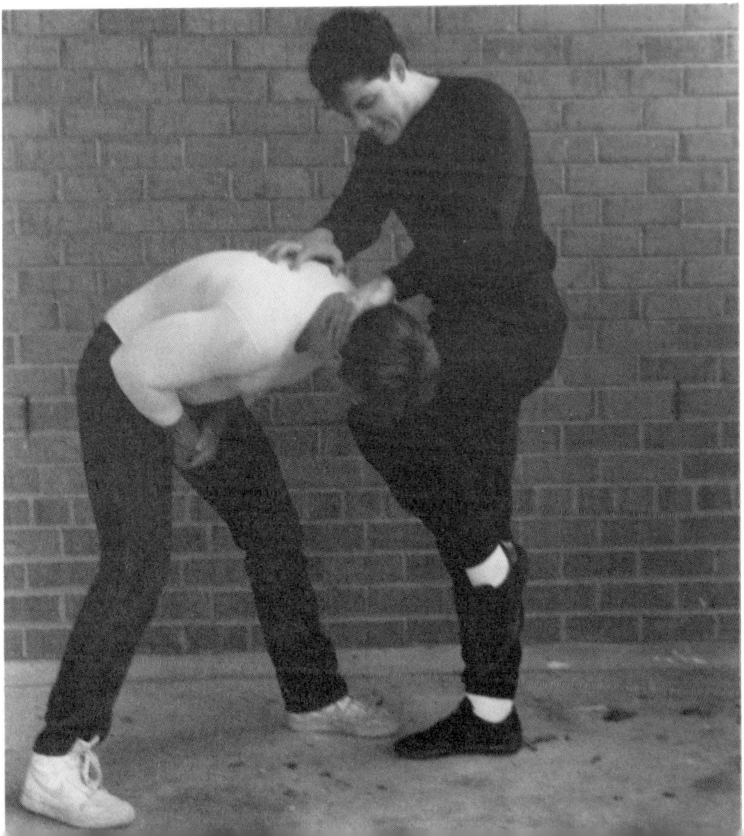

Defending Against a Full-Nelson Headlock

Franco is attacked from behind and is placed in a full nelson. Without a moment's hesitation, he quickly stomps on the opponent's foot to loosen his lock.

The Defensive Structure

Franco then reaches back, grabs hold of the attacker's index finger, and pulls back forcefully. The adversary is forced to release his lock. Franco is now able to control him.

While still applying pressure on the opponent's finger, Franco drives a vertical knee to the groin. He then follows with a lead hook to the head.

Defending Against a Throat Choke (pinned on the floor)

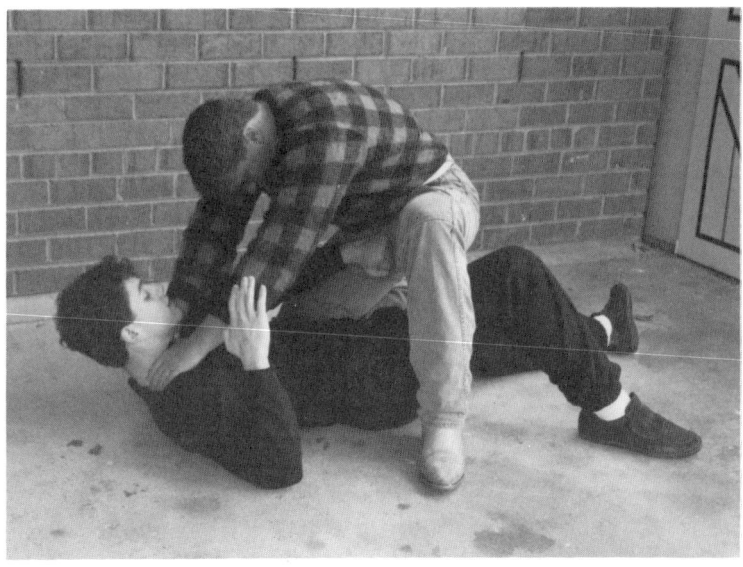

Franco is forced to the ground and is being choked. Before the attacker can apply pressure, the martial artist strikes his groin to loosen his hold.

Once the opponent loosens his choke, Franco attacks his eyes with a double thumb gouge.

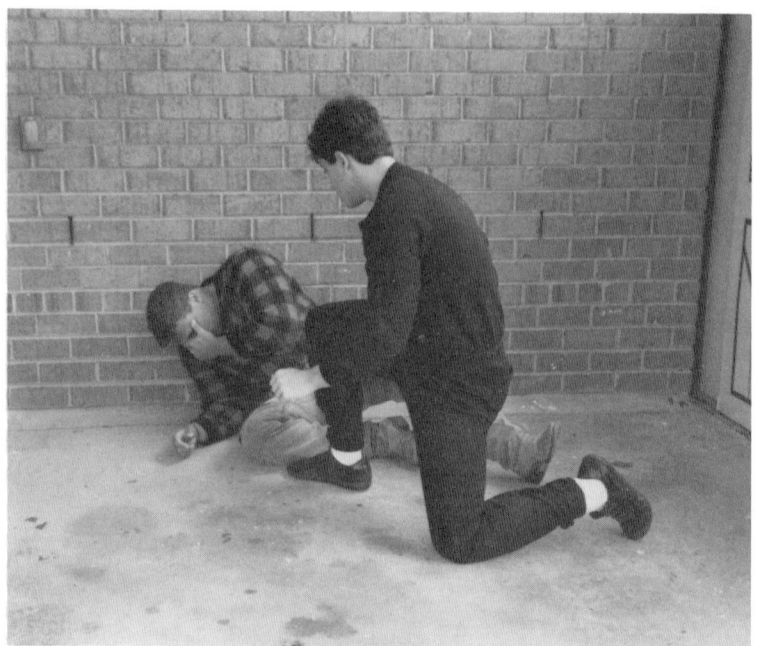
The dangerous altercation is quickly over.

The Defensive Structure

Defending Against a Throat Choke (while standing)

Franco is confronted by a threatening opponent.

The assailant then grabs him by the throat.

Franco quickly counters with a finger jab to the eyes.

He then finishes the attacker off with a hook kick to the knee.

The Defensive Structure
Defending Against a Shirt Grab

The opponent grabs Franco's shirt and begins to threaten him.

Franco quickly traps his opponent's grabbing hand while simultaneously executing a finger jab to his eyes.

The opponent releases his grab. Franco then throws a rear cross to the nose.

The Defensive Structure

Defending Against a Shoulder Grab

The assailant grabs Franco by the shoulder.

The martial artist traps his grabbing hand and simultaneously counters with a rear cross.

Defending Against a Rear Arm Lock

The opponent grabs Franco's left arm and puts it into a lock.

Before the opponent can apply any pressure, Franco counters with a reverse elbow to the ribs.

The Defensive Structure

He follows up with a kick to the knee.

The attacker falls to the pavement in pain, and Franco moves in to finish him off.

Conclusion

We live in a modern society infested with crime and violence. It is a place where the traditional martial arts are not functional for self-defense. The classical techniques that they advocate are simply too ornamental and impractical for the grim realities of the street. It is time to move on to a new generation of martial arts based on effective and efficient techniques that can be employed against any opponent at any time and in any place.

Contemporary Fighting Arts is a modern martial art adapted to today's realities. Its primary objective is to produce a complete martial artist who can handle any situation. By absorbing the physical, mental, and spiritual elements of the art, the practitioner will acquire self-enlightenment and a greater understanding of the principles of unarmed combat.